EYEWITNESS ● JUNIORS
AMAZING
SPIDERS

EYEWITNESS ● JUNIORS

AMAZING SPIDERS

WRITTEN BY
ALEXANDRA PARSONS

PHOTOGRAPHED BY
JERRY YOUNG

DORLING KINDERSLEY
London • New York • Moscow • Sydney

DK

A DORLING KINDERSLEY BOOK

Editor Scott Steadman
Designers Ann Cannings and Margo Beamish-White
Senior art editor Jacquie Gulliver
Editorial director Sue Unstead
Art director Anne-Marie Bulat

Special photography by Jerry Young
Illustrations by Mark Iley and Poly Noakes
Animals supplied by Trevor Smith's Animal World
Editorial consultants The staff of the Natural History Museum, London

Published in Great Britain by
Dorling Kindersley Limited
9 Henrietta Street, London WC2E 8PS

Paperback edition
2 4 6 8 10 9 7 5 3 1

Copyright © 1990, 1998 Dorling Kindersley Limited, London

Visit us on the World Wide Web at
http://www.dk.com

A CIP catalogue record for this book is available from the British Library.

ISBN 0-7513-5761-8

Colour reproduction by Colourscan, Singapore
Printed and bound in Singapore by Imago

Contents

What is a spider?

There are about 30,000 different kinds of spider in the world. They may look scary but most spiders can't harm people. They are important in the balance of nature because they eat so many insects.

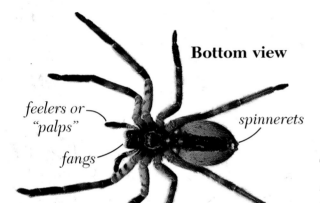

Bottom view

feelers or "palps"

spinnerets

fangs

Terrible table manners

All spiders kill and eat other animals. They use their fearsome fangs to catch and hold their victims – usually insects. The spider then covers its prey in strong digestive juices. These make a mush of the insect's insides so the spider can suck it dry.

Poor Arachne!

Spiders belong to a group of animals called arachnids (*uh-rack-nids*). They are named after Arachne, a girl in a Greek legend who won a weaving contest with the goddess Athena. The goddess was so angry that Arachne killed herself. Athena was sorry and turned Arachne's body into a spider, so she could keep on weaving.

Spiders have eight legs with six joints each – that's 48 knees!

Spiders don't have bones – instead their insides are protected by a hard layer of skin called a cuticle.

Eye spy
We have two eyes, but most spiders have two rows of four eyes. That makes eight.

fine silk thread from spinneret

spinneret

Spider webbing
Spiders spin their silk with tiny organs called spinnerets. The silk starts as a sticky liquid which hardens in the air to form a very light, but very strong thread.

The two main parts of a spider's body are the joined head and chest at the front and the abdomen at the back.

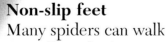

Non-slip feet
Many spiders can walk up walls and across ceilings because they have special grip-pads on their feet.

Spare skin
As a spider grows, its hard outer skin becomes too tight. It sheds the whole skin, first cracking it open on the back and then pulling out its legs.

Friends of the Earth

The most common spiders of all are the house spider and the garden spider. If you see them, don't kill them. They help keep your house and garden free of bugs.

Sticky centre
The garden spider spins a beautiful spiral web designed to catch flying insects. The centre is made of a special sticky silk so insects that fly into it can't fly out.

The large palps are very sensitive to vibrations in the spider's web.

Munch, munch!
There are billions and billions of spiders in the world. If every spider ate just one insect a day for a year and you piled up all those insects in one spot, they would weigh as much as 50 million people!

Two of this garden spider's eyes are on top of its head.

Perfect pet
The house spider makes a good pet. You won't have to feed it too often – a fly a day is more than enough. A spider needs water, so give it a damp sponge to suck.

Close to mother
Some female spiders lay their eggs in a silk cocoon. The spider carries this with her, scurrying around her web with the ball of silk hanging from her abdomen.

Yuk!
Little Miss Muffet was a real little girl. Her father, Thomas Muffet, was a spider expert who used to make his daughter eat mashed spiders when she was ill. This was a common remedy for colds two hundred years ago!

The untidy spider
The house spider is a messy eater. Its web looks like a dirty little hammock. It spits out any bits of insect that are too hard to eat and leaves them for someone else to clean up.

A spider's skin is covered in oil so it won't stick to its own silk.

The most likely place to find a house spider is in your bath – they go there in search of water.

Strange decorations
Many garden spiders have beautiful patterns on their backs. Scientists still don't know how they help the spiders. They may be used to attract mates.

Giant, hairy spiders

This spider is a Chilean red-leg and it is one of the biggest and hairiest spiders in the world. It is so big that it can eat mice and small birds.

Seeing and feeling

Spiders may have a lot of eyes, but most can't see very well. To help them find their way, they have very sensitive hairs on their legs and feelers.

Dance the tarantella

Not all large, hairy spiders are tarantulas. The real tarantula is a big, poisonous spider from Italy. People used to believe that dancing was the only cure for the spider's bite. The dance became known as the tarantella.

Hairy scary

When it's attacked, this spider will tear the prickly hairs off its back and fling them at its attacker.

Eek!

Being terrified of spiders is called arachnophobia (*ah-rack-no-foe-bee-uh*).

*Strong legs
used to dig
burrows*

Little and large
The world's smallest spider lives on the Pacific island of Samoa. It is so small that it would fit on the full stop at the end of this sentence. The biggest spider of all lurks in the jungles of South America. It measures about 25 cm with its legs stretched out. That's about the size of a dinner plate.

Old age pensioners
Female tarantulas have been known to live for over 25 years. Most males die by the age of nine or ten.

*Most male
spiders have
smaller bodies
than females,
though their legs
are just as long.*

Facts about fangs
Most spiders have fangs that swing together, grasping their prey like a pair of pliers. But big spiders like tarantulas have downward-pointing fangs for pinning down their lunch.

Water spiders

Spiders that live in or on the water still need to breathe air. One water spider traps bubbles of air in an underwater web, where it lives and lays its eggs.

The diving bell

The water spider spins a web in the shape of a bell underneath the water. It fills the bell with a bubble of air and anchors it to a piece of water weed. This air pocket is the spider's underwater home.

You can tell a raft spider by the pale bands on the sides of its dark body.

Refilling the tanks

When its underwater web needs more air, the hard-working water spider goes up to the surface and traps tiny bubbles in the hairs of its body. Then it zips back home to let go of the air bubbles inside its tiny web.

Like most spiders, the raft spider has tiny claws at the end of its feet.

The crafty raft spider

This spider lives by the water's edge. It's quite big, but it can walk on water without sinking. It does this by spreading its legs wide and taking quick, gentle steps.

A new wardrobe

Like all spiders, the raft spider sheds its skin as it gets bigger. When the growing spider crawls out of its old skin, or cuticle, it is covered in a new, soft skin. It leaves the old cuticle behind and sits in the sun for a few hours until the new skin hardens.

New legs

If a spider loses a leg (and they quite often do), it can simply grow a new one.

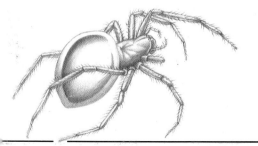

Gone fishing

The swamp spider lives on the surface of the water, where it catches and eats tiny minnows. To attract its prey, the spider dabbles its feet in the water. When the unsuspecting fish rise to the surface, the spider pounces and in go the fangs.

Jack-in-the-box

Trapdoor spiders and purse-web spiders live in burrows. Each spider builds a silken trap around the mouth of its den. When a tasty meal strolls by, the spider leaps out like a jack-in-the-box.

Lair with a lid
A trapdoor spider spends most of its time in its underground burrow, waiting for a bug to pass its door.

The spare room
Some trapdoor spiders dig out several "rooms" in their burrows. One will be a dining room, one may be a nursery, and one will be a safe place to shelter during a flood.

This spider has shiny armour plating on its head and chest to protect its insides. The velvety abdomen is much softer.

Neighbours
Burrowing spiders like the trapdoor spider live on their own, one to a burrow. Several spiders may live close together but they don't do it to be neighbourly – they do it because the area is good for building burrows.

Bugs in the pantry

If spiders catch an insect when they're not hungry, they will poison it without killing it and wrap it up in silk. Then they can be sure of a nice fresh meal whenever they feel peckish.

Built-in plug

One kind of trap-door spider has a body shaped like the nose cone of a rocket. When it is chased, it bolts down its hole and plugs up the entrance with its hard, flat bottom.

Trapdoor spiders are mainly found in warm, tropical regions – this one is from the southern United States.

A silken prison

The female purse-web spider lives in a silken pouch that spills out of her burrow. When an insect stumbles on her trap, she slices the pouch open and sinks in her fangs.

Jumpers and spitters

Not all spiders catch their meals in webs. Some jump on their prey, and others spit out a sticky net of poison.

What muscles!
A jumping spider can leap 40 times its body length.

The legs of a jumping spider are short and very, very strong.

Safety rope
The jumping spider hunts insects like a cat hunts mice. But before it jumps on its prey, the spider anchors itself to the ground with a silk thread.

Slow but sure
The spitting spider moves very slowly, but it can even catch a speedy fly. The spider spits out a net of poison and glue that takes the insect completely by surprise, pinning it to the ground.

A high jumper

Jumping spiders are found all over the world, from Europe to the Amazon. There is even a type of jumping spider that lives near the top of Mount Everest, the world's highest mountain. This hairy specimen is from Egypt.

Look before you leap

A jumping spider has wonderful eyesight – for a spider. It has two huge eyes in the middle of its head, four more on top, and one on each side. The spider hardly has to move its head to see in all directions.

Homebody

The spitting spider is not very fond of fresh air or playing in the garden. It prefers to live indoors close to people.

The specialists

Many spiders like to do things their own way.
Some are very choosy about their food, and
others have learned some pretty
sneaky ways to catch their prey.

Neat trick!

Some crab spiders live on flowers that are the
same colour as they are. They pretend to be a
petal and sit there perfectly still, just waiting for
an insect to walk right into their open arms.

Twirling for moths

The bolas spider is particularly fond of
moths, and has worked out a clever way
of catching them. First it squirts
out a special scent that
attracts the insects. The
spider then takes a thread
of silk with a sticky blob on the end and
twirls it around in the air. Curious moths
fly towards it and thwack! They're stuck!

A lonely life

Spiders don't make
friends. If you put
two together in a
box, they will
fight to the death.

A living twig

The net-casting spider lives in trees in the jungle. Some bigger animals would like to eat it, but it has a wonderful disguise – when it lies flat against a branch, it is almost impossible to see.

This crab spider has a poisonous bite that is deadly to insects but harmless to humans.

Nice throw!

The net-casting spider has its very own way of catching prey. It spins a sticky net which it holds between its front legs – ready to throw over passing insects.

Any old silk

Some people just won't throw old silk away! Neither will some spiders. They eat their old webs. Then they turn the old silk into new inside their bodies.

Cockroach control

It's not the bananas that banana spiders love, but the cockroaches that live on them! If we wanted to, we could even use banana spiders to kill these nasty creatures for us.

Black and deadly

A bite from a female black widow spider could kill you. Luckily she hides away from people most of the time. She bites only if her web is disturbed.

An imposter!

There is a perfectly harmless spider called the false black widow. It looks just the same as the deadly black widow except that it has no red patch on its underside.

A dangerous mission

Courting a female is a very risky business for the male black widow. Because he is so much smaller than she is, he has to be careful that she doesn't mistake him for a juicy insect and gobble him up for lunch.

You can easily tell a real black widow by its red markings.

Bearing gifts

One way for the male to avoid being eaten by his lady is to bring her a present. A nice fresh bug all wrapped up in silk often does the trick.

Deadly shy

The black widow is a shy little spider that doesn't like to fight. That's why it has such deadly poison. If a great big scorpion or lizard gets stuck in its web, all the spider has to do is nip the scorpion's leg, stand back, and wham! Lunch is ready.

Bringing up baby

The black widow glues her egg sac to a branch and waits for the eggs to hatch. The baby spiders will have nothing to eat but each other until they are big enough to build webs of their own. Out of 100 baby spiders, maybe 25 will survive.

Funnel of death

The Australian funnelweb spider is one of the world's deadliest. It is big and black, with hairy legs and huge fangs so strong they can pierce bone.

Poison fangs

All spiders have poisonous bites, but some are more poisonous than others. Luckily scientists have now made special medicines that can cure people who have been badly bitten.

Hard to kill

Sprays that would kill other spiders just make funnel-webs angry.

Silky sheets

The funnelweb lives underground in the cool and damp. It lines its burrow with sheets of silk and sleeps through the winter.

Number one

The deadliest spider in the whole world is the Brazilian wandering spider.

Trip trap

As you may have guessed, the funnelweb's web is shaped like a funnel. The narrow end of the funnel leads into the spider's burrow, and the wide end lies around the entrance. The spider spins fine triplines running out from the web, so it can tell if a tasty insect, frog, or lizard is strolling by.

Funnelwebs have thick hairs on their legs, but none at all on their bodies.

25

The weavers

Orb weaver spiders spin beautiful, intricate webs. You can tell an orb web because it is shaped like a target and strung between two supports.

Can spiders fly?
Spiders don't have wings, so they cannot actually fly. But some tiny spiders get blown about by the wind. Using silk threads like little parachutes, they can travel on the breeze for hundreds of miles.

Speedy spider
The fastest spider in the world can run 330 times its own body length in 10 seconds. A person can only manage 50 times his body length in that time.

Silk or steel?
If you made a steel thread as fine as a thread of spider silk, the silk would be three times stronger.

Young spinners

Each kind of spider builds its own kind of web. The moment a spider hatches from its egg, it knows how to spin a certain pattern, just as you were born knowing how to cry and how to suck.

To spin its web, the black orb weaver spider uses a thread of silk so long it would wrap around this book 50 times.

First aid

If you cut yourself, try putting a clean spider's web on the wound to stop the bleeding and help the cut to heal.

The bristles on a spider's legs help it feel vibrations in the air – or on its web.

Fishing nets

There is a spider called *Nephila* that lives in very hot countries. The webs it makes are so thick and so strong that the local people collect them and use them as fishing nets.

How to spin a web

It takes a spider about an hour to spin an orb web like this. The fine silk thread looks delicate, but it can hold 4,000 times the spider's own weight!

1 First the spider spins a thread between two supports – helped, perhaps, by a breeze that wafts the thread across. Then it spins another and dangles from the middle.

3 Then the spider spins round and round in a spiral, working slowly out from the middle.

4 Finally, it spirals back into the centre and sits and waits there for an insect to fly by.

Spiders have to repair their fragile webs all the time because careless insects keep flying into them.

2 Next it drops a new thread to make a Y-shape, and spins more threads from the centre to the edge.

Trip wire

Spiders often lie in wait – with one leg on a "signal thread". When an unsuspecting victim lands in the web, the thread shakes. Instantly, the spider pounces.

Index